'amme
roject
ement
ıry

Pocketbook

Central Computer and Telecommunications Agency

London: The Stationery Office

Contents

Introduction

PROMPT II was introduced as a Government standard for project management, supported by CCTA, in January 1983. It provided an organised but flexible management and control framework within which a product could be correctly specified, designed, developed and installed. In March 1989 the name PRINCE was adopted to differentiate the Government version, following the introduction of a number of new features.

PRINCE 2 was launched on October 1st, 1996. The new version has a number of improvements and is designed to be applicable to all types and size of project.

The basic principles of PROMPT have not been changed, but the standard has been strengthened in such areas as the management of risk and details of the steps of the project management process.

The full details of PRINCE 2 are to be found in the PRINCE 2 manual, published by The Stationery Office, ISBN 0 11 330855 8. This Pocketbook is produced as an aide-memoire and handy reference for the trained PRINCE practitioner, who is assumed to be familiar with the method and the terminology.

- QUALITY IN A PROJECT ENVIRONMENT
- MANAGEMENT OF RISK
- CHANGE
- CONFIGURATION MANAGEMENT
- THE PROJECT MANAGEMENT PROCESS

THE CUSTOMER/SUPPLIER ENVIRONMENT

PRINCE 2 is defined in terms of a Customer/Supplier environment. This assumes that within any project there are various groups of people with an interest in the project and its outcome, including:

- customers who have commissioned the work and will be benefiting from the end results
- users who will use or operate the final product (the customer and user may be the same group of people in some situations)
- suppliers who are providing specialist resources and/or skills to the project, or are providing goods and services
- sub-contractors who provide products or services to the supplier.

PRINCE 2 accepts that the customer and supplier may come from separately managed areas and typically from commercially separate organisations.

APPLYING PRINCE 2

PRINCE 2 is designed to be used on any type of project in any environment. It contains a complete set of concepts and project management processes which are the minimum requirements for a properly run and managed project. However, the way in which PRINCE 2 is applied to each project will vary considerably according to such constraints as size, risk cost and duration. Tailoring the method to suit the circumstances of a particular project is critical to its successful use. The philosophy behind each part of PRINCE 2 can be applied to even the smallest of projects.

The Project Management Process

PRINCE 2 documents all the project management steps in a process model. This has eight processes which describe the steps to take from the inception of a project to its close.

Any project run under PRINCE 2 will address each of these processes in some form, but the processes do not represent a sequential step-by-step guide to project management. Many of the steps are iterative, some can be done in parallel with others, and each process is scaleable according to the needs of the project. The key to successful use of this process model is to ask the question 'How extensively should this process be applied on this project?'

STARTING UP A PROJECT (SU)

This is a pre-project process, designed to do five things:
- ensure that the necessary authority for undertaking the project exists
- ensure that sufficient information about the project objectives, scope and constraints is available
- design and appoint the project management team
- decide on the approach to be used to provide a solution
- create the initiation stage plan.

Corporate or Programme Management

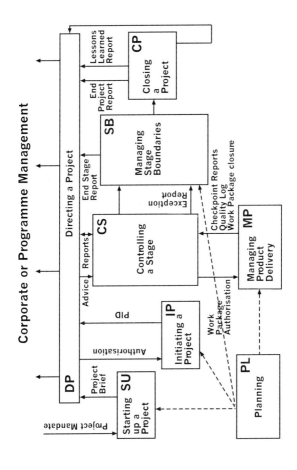

Directing a Project

DP — Directing a Project

SU — Starting up a Project

IP — Initiating a Project

CS — Controlling a Stage

SB — Managing Stage Boundaries

CP — Closing a Project

MP — Managing Product Delivery

PL — Planning

Project Mandate

Project Brief

Authorisation

PID

Advice

Reports

End Stage Report

Exception Report

End Project Report

Lessons Learned Report

Checkpoint Reports
Quality Log
Work Package closure

Work Package Authorisation

DIRECTING A PROJECT (DP)

This process covers the duties of the Project Board and runs from the start-up of a project to its closure.

The key processes for the Project Board break into five main areas.

- Approving the project brief and authorising initiation.
- Authorising the Project Initiation Document at the end of initiation.
- Checking project status at the end of each stage before authorising continuation to the next stage.
- Providing advice and guidance as requested and reacting to exception situations.
- Confirming project closure.

INITIATING A PROJECT (IP)

This process is aimed at laying down a firm and accepted foundation for the project.

- Check that everyone involved understands the scope and objectives of the project.
- Check that a suitable business case exists for the project.
- Check that the project has been adequately planned and costed.
- Check that the risks are acceptable.
- Encourage the Project Board to take ownership of the project.
- Obtain commitment from the Project Board of the resources for the next stage.

CONTROLLING A STAGE (CS)

This process gives the steps to handle day-to-day management of the project. Use of the steps will be cyclic, consisting of:

- authorising work to be done
- monitoring events
- taking any necessary corrective action
- taking delivery of completed products
- capturing and acting on all project issues.

MANAGING PRODUCT DELIVERY (MP)

This process is designed for Team Managers:

- negotiating and accepting work packages from the Project Manager
- ensuring that the work is done
- reporting on progress and quality work done
- ensuring that completed products meet quality criteria
- obtaining approval for completed products.

MANAGING STAGE BOUNDARIES (SB)

This process covers the Project Manager's steps needed at the end of a stage to provide the Project Board with the information necessary for it to decide whether to continue to the next stage. It is also used when producing an exception plan.

- Report on the delivery of all expected products.
- Collate information relating to the continuing viability of the project.
- Re-assess the risk situation.
- The next stage plan.

CLOSING A PROJECT (CP)

A clear and unambiguous end to a project is required, whether it is a successful completion or early termination. The sub-processes and steps are to prepare input to the Project Board to obtain its confirmation that the project may close.

- Report on fulfilment of the Project Initiation Document's objectives.
- Confirm that the customer is satisfied and that the relevant group(s) are ready to take the final product into its operational life.
- Recommend any follow-up actions.
- Record any useful lessons learned.

PLANNING (PL)

Planning is a common process, used by several of the other processes. It describes the construction of any level of plan. The PRINCE 2 planning process and framework can be applied to any type of project.

The process begins by making decisions on any planning tools, estimation methods, levels of plan and monitoring methods to be used. Then the PRINCE 2 product-based planning technique is used to define and analyse the products.

The technique has three steps.

- Create a Product Breakdown Structure which identifies the business products plus the management and quality products to be produced.
- Write Product Descriptions which describe the products in terms of their purpose, composition, derivation and quality requirements and ensure that these descriptions are fully understood and agreed by everyone involved.
- Draw a Product Flow Diagram which shows the logical order of creation of these products and any dependencies between the products.

Further steps in the process identify the required activities to produce the products, estimate the effort and duration for each activity, calculate the cost of the plan, assess the inherent risks and identify the management control points needed.

The whole planning process is intended to be cyclic, and several iterations of its steps are normally needed.

Introduction to the PRINCE 2 Components

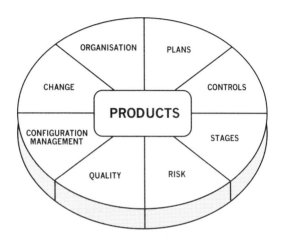

The components of PRINCE 2 focus on the products which the project has to deliver. The components are used by the processes. The processes link the components together and show how and when they are used in the project.

Organisation

However small or large the project, there needs to be general agreement on:
• who says what is needed
• who provides the budget
• who provides the development resources
• who authorises any changes
• who manages the day-to-day work
• who defines any standards to be met.

In a small project the answer to a number of these questions may be the same person. In a large project a number of people may be the answer to one of these questions. The PRINCE 2 solution to this need for flexibility is to provide a project management structure consisting of a number of ROLES. A role can be allocated to one person, shared between a number of people or combined with another role.

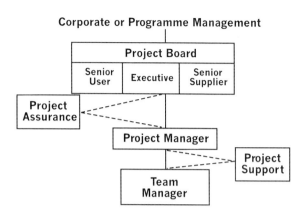

Corporate or Programme Management

PROJECT BOARD

Within the constraints defined by corporate or
programme management, the Project Board

at the start of the project:

• agrees on the Project Manager's responsibilities and
objectives
• decides how the task of project assurance is to be
carried out
• confirms project tolerances with the appropriate body
of senior management
• approves the Project Initiation Document

as the project progresses:

• gives direction and guidance

- reviews the project status at the end of each completed stage and approves progress to the next stage
- checks that the project is still on track to meet the defined business need
- reviews and approves any exception plans
- approves changes to the product specification
- reports to corporate or programme management
- may recommend project termination

at the end of the project:
- ensures that all expected products have been delivered satisfactorily
- confirms that operational and support groups are prepared to take responsibility for the product
- authorises project closure.

The Project Board consists of three roles, those of Executive, Senior User and Senior Supplier.

Executive

The Executive is ultimately accountable for the project to corporate or programme management. The Executive has to ensure that the project is value for money and ensure a cost-conscious approach to the project, balancing the demands of business, the users and suppliers.

Senior User
The Senior User is accountable for ensuring that requirements are fully and accurately specified, making sure that what is produced is fit for its purpose and for ensuring that the solution meets user needs within the constraints of the business case.

Senior Supplier
This role represents the interests of those designing, developing, facilitating, procuring and implementing the project products. The Senior Supplier must have the authority to commit or acquire the required supplier resources. In a third party contract the Senior Supplier would possibly be a management representative of the third party or the customer's contracts manager.

PROJECT MANAGER
The Project Manager:
- prepares project and stage plans
- obtains Project Board approval of plans
- defines responsibilities and allocates work within the project
- monitors and controls progress within the tolerances laid down by the Project Board
- negotiates the performance of work packages with Team Managers
- schedules stage control points
- liaises with the project assurance roles
- prepares reports for the Project Board

- presents project status at the end of every stage
- enforces quality and change control procedures
- ensures the maintenance of risk, quality and issue logs
- prepares any reports required about situations which threaten the set tolerances
- prepares any exception plans required.

TEAM MANAGER

This is an optional role. It is likely to be used in larger projects where teams of different skills or knowledge are required. It may also be used where the Project Manager is part of the customer organisation and work is being done by a third party.

The role:
- negotiates work packages with the Project Manager
- plans and allocates work within the team
- monitors team progress and costs, and initiates any necessary corrective action
- reports progress to the Project Manager
- maintains details of the quality checks performed
- reports any project issues
- liaises with any appointed assurance roles.

PROJECT ASSURANCE

Project assurance is a check, independent of the Project Manager, that the project continues to meet its specification, the required technical standards and its business case.

In PRINCE 2 project assurance is a responsibility of each Project Board member. It can be delegated if warranted by the size or complexity of the project. Assurance responsibilities can be viewed under the following headings:

Business

- Focus on the business case is maintained
- Risks are being controlled
- Maintenance of liaison between customer and supplier
- Monitoring expenditure and schedule
- Ensuring that the project remains viable
- Ensuring that the project gives 'value for money'
- Fit with company or programme strategy

User

- user needs and expectations are being met or managed
- an acceptable solution is being developed

Specialist

- Liaison is being maintained between customer and supplier
- The needs of specialist interests are being observed
- The scope of the project is not increasing unnoticed
- The required technical standards are being used, used correctly and are working.

PROJECT SUPPORT

The Project Manager may need administrative help. This may stem from the sheer volume of work to be done or the mandated use of certain tools where the Project Manager has insufficient expertise, such as in planning and control or configuration management.

A Project Support Office is one which supports one or more projects with such skills and can be a good way of providing scarce skills in a cost-effective manner.

Plans

Plan

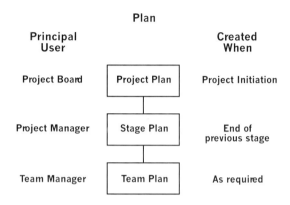

Principal User		Created When
Project Board	Project Plan	Project Initiation
Project Manager	Stage Plan	End of previous stage
Team Manager	Team Plan	As required

In PRINCE 2 the Project Plan is the only mandatory plan.
Most projects will also need Stage Plans. If the project
uses a number of teams, there may be a need for Team
Plans. The diagram above shows the levels of PRINCE 2
plans.

The **Project Plan** is a high-level plan showing the key
deliverables and major control points of the project, such
as stage boundaries. It summarises the resource
requirements and costs, and is used by the Project Board
as a baseline against which to monitor actual costs and
progress stage by stage.

A **Stage Plan** contains the level of detail needed to be an adequate basis for day-to-day control by the Project Manager. Each Stage Plan is produced near the end of the previous stage.

Team Plans may be used when there are a number of teams working in a stage, especially if those teams are from different skill groups or work for external suppliers.

Part way through a stage the Project Manager may be asked by the Project Board to produce an **Exception Plan**. This would follow an exception report describing a forecast deviation beyond the tolerance levels agreed for the Stage Plan. The format of an Exception Plan is the same as that of the Stage Plan. An Exception Plan replaces the remainder of the Stage Plan and shows the work and resources necessary to react to the deviation.

CONTENTS OF A PLAN

A plan is a document, framed in accordance with a pre-defined scheme or method, a design of how identified targets for deliverables, timescales, costs and quality can be met. PRINCE 2 expects a graphical summary of the plan, e.g. a bar chart, to be supported by a specific format of text, as follows:

- graphical summary
- plan description
- prerequisites and assumptions

- external dependencies
- risks
- tolerances

PREPARING A PLAN

PRINCE 2 has a product-based approach to preparing a plan. This has three steps; preparing a Product Breakdown Structure, writing Product Descriptions and creating a Product Flow Diagram.

All PRINCE 2 products fall into one of three categories.

- MANAGEMENT PRODUCTS
  These are produced as a result of organising, planning and controlling the project. They include the Project Initiation Document, job descriptions, plans, reports and Project Board approvals.
- QUALITY PRODUCTS
  This category includes all documents which establish the required quality of a product, track the implementation of the necessary quality check actions or record project issues and the action taken.
- SPECIALIST PRODUCTS
  These consist of all the products defined in the project brief, including all the final products and the interim products, such as specification and design documents.

PRODUCT BREAKDOWN STRUCTURE

The PRINCE 2 Product Breakdown Structure is a hierarchy of products required to complete a given project. At each level in the hierarchy, products are the total components of the level above. The hierarchy contains the management, quality and specialist products.

The number of levels in the hierarchy is consistent with the level of detail required from the plan.

PRODUCT DESCRIPTIONS

Product Descriptions are written for each product identified in the Product Breakdown Structure. They describe the purpose, composition and quality criteria, and confirm understanding of the product.

Writing a Product Description enhances understanding of the required product, defines to both the developer and the checker the testing / quality assessment required and gives a feel for the resources and timescale needed for its creation.

PRODUCT FLOW DIAGRAM

The Product Flow Diagram shows the logical sequence in which products need to be developed. It consists of all the products shown in the Product Breakdown Structure, including all three categories. Identifying the derivation of each product from previous products and the quality checking process required prepares the way for production of an activity network.

Controls

PRINCE 2 provides a series of controls to support
'management by exception'. That is, having agreed a
plan, no management intervention is required until that
plan is complete unless an exception arises. An
'exception' is identified by setting deviation limits
(tolerances) to the plan. Any change which would result
in the project or stage going beyond these limits would
constitute an exception.

STAGES

The division of a project into stages is to permit the
Project Board to set a number of control points beyond
which the Project Manager may not proceed without the
Project Board having the opportunity to re-examine the
viability of the project.

Two different types of stage can be considered,
management stages and *technical* stages. Management
stages equate to commitment of resources and authority
to spend. Technical stages are typified by the use of a
particular set of specialist skills. PRINCE 2 uses
management stages, since these will form the basis of the
planning and control processes described throughout the
method. To do otherwise runs the risk of the project
being driven by the specialist teams instead of the
customer's management.

The Project Board only commits to one stage at a time (See End Stage Assessment), thus providing one reason why stage plans are not produced until the end of the previous stage.

START-UP

At the outset of a project the Project Board is appointed and approves the resource and time expenditure needed to produce the Project Initiation Document.

PROJECT INITIATION

This is a Project Board control point to:
- review and agree the Project Initiation Document
- ensure that the project objectives are understood and agreed by all
- ensure that a valid business case exists for the project
- review the risks and ensure that proposals to meet them are adequate.

The Project Initiation Document (PID) is the basis of the 'contract' for the project between the Project Board and the Project Manager. It contains sections on:
- background to the project
- project definition
- acceptance criteria
- assumptions
- initial business case
- project organisation structure
- project quality plan

- initial Project Plan
- project controls
- exception process
- initial risk log
- contingency plans
- project filing structure.

TOLERANCES
These are the amounts by which the Project Manager may deviate from a Stage Plan without having to produce an Exception Report for the Project Board. Tolerance limits are set by the Project Board for cost and schedule.

Corporate or programme management set project tolerance limits for the Project Board to define its flexibility in decision-making before referring problems back to higher management.

CHECKPOINTS
Regular team meetings and reports to the Project Manager on progress, problems and future expected targets.

HIGHLIGHT REPORTS
Regular reports from the Project Manager to the Project Board on progress against the Stage Plan, current or potential problems and expected events in the near future. These are based on and consolidate the checkpoint reports.

END STAGE ASSESSMENT

Project Board mandatory control point to review:

- actual completion of a stage against the Stage Plan
- the status of the Project Plan
- the status of the business case
- the status of risks
- the next Stage Plan (and approve it if satisfied).

EXCEPTION REPORT

This is a report sent by the Project Manager to the Project Board when the tolerances for the project or a stage are forecast to be exceeded. The reason for the deviation may be a major change to requirements or a failure by the project to meet its planned costs or schedule or to fulfil some part of the requirements.

MID STAGE ASSESSMENT

This is an unplanned Project Board control point at which it would consider an Exception Plan.

PROJECT CLOSURE

This is a mandatory control point for the Project Board, usually a meeting. It is often combined with the End Stage Assessment of the final stage.

It:

- confirms that all expected products have been delivered and accepted
- checks that any issues raised have been resolved or documented for passage to the appropriate body

- checks that any lessons learned have been documented and ensures their passage to the relevant group
- approves any plan for post implementation review
- approves the end project report
- authorises formal closure of the project.

PRINCE 2 CONTROL SUMMARY

Control	Objective	Frequency	Prepared by	For
Project Initiation Meeting	Approve Initiation Stage Plan	At start of initiation / end of start-up (May not need to be formal meeting)	Project Manager	Project Board
Project Initiation Document	Document agreement on the what, why, who, how and when of the project	At the end of initiation stage	Project Manager	Project Board
End Stage Assessment	Review project status and approve next stage plan	End of each stage	Project Manager	Project Board
Checkpoint	Team progress report	Regular intervals, often weekly	Team Manager	Project Manager
Highlight Report	Stage status report	Intervals agreed with Project Board, e.g. monthly	Project Manager	Project Board
Project Issue	Describe a change to requirements or problem	As required	Anyone	Project Manager
Exception Report	Description of a forecast deviation beyond tolerance levels and the options open	When tolerance levels threatened	Project Manager	Project Board
Mid Stage Assessment	Review Exception Plan	After an Exception Report	Project Manager	Project Board
Tolerance	permitted plan deviation	For each stage plan	Project Manager under Project Board guidance	Project Manager
Project Closure	To confirm that the project has met its objectives	At the end of project	Project Manager	Project Board

Change

PRINCE 2 contains a change control mechanism which is capable of capturing all types of issue and tracking them to completion. The mechanism is designed to fit in with all other PRINCE 2 controls, such as configuration management and Exception Reports. PRINCE 2 is also compatible with many other change control procedures which may be already in place in organisations.

All changes are treated as types of project issue and are handled through the same change control approach.

Project issues can be:

- REQUESTS FOR CHANGE
  One type of issue is any proposed modification to the agreed specification or acceptance criteria.

- OFF-SPECIFICATIONS
  Another type of issue records a current or forecast failure to meet part of the agreed specification or an acceptance criterion.

- PROJECT ISSUES
  The third type of issue may be simply a question, a concern or anything which does not fall into the two types above. These can usually be answered directly and do not lead to extra work.

Every issue is recorded in the issue log, which allocates a unique number and records the author, date, priority and type of project issue. A copy of the project issue is returned to the author to acknowledge its receipt and an updated copy sent to the author whenever extra information is added or the status of the project issue changes.

If the project issue is not simply a question which can be satisfied with an immediate answer, an impact analysis is carried out, after which the priority is reviewed by the Senior User role (or someone delegated). The general procedure is for the Senior User role to decide which changes should be implemented, persuade the other Project Board roles, then get the Project Manager to incorporate these in the project. This often requires the production of an Exception Report by the Project Manager, leading to a review of the project and stage plans, the business case and risk situation and causing the creation of an Exception Plan.

Changes can be implemented, rejected, sent back for further information or held over for possible later implementation by staff supporting the final product.

As off-specifications represent some kind of failure on the part of the project to deliver what was expected, there is far more pressure on the Project Manager to solve this type of project issue within the tolerance margins of the stage or project.

Configuration Management

The assets of a project are the products which it delivers. These are not only the specialist or business products, but also the management and quality products, such as plans, approvals and the results of quality checks. The name for the combined set of these assets is the configuration. The purpose of configuration management is to identify, track and protect the project's products.

Configuration management consists of four basic functions:
- **identification** - identifying and describing all the products required to be delivered by the project
- **control** - the ability to agree and 'freeze' configuration items and then to make changes only with the agreement of appropriate named authorities. Once a product has been approved, the motto is 'nothing moves, nothing changes without authorisation'.
- **status accounting** - the recording and reporting of the information about a product, and the ability to track a product through all the changes in its status
- **verification** - a series of reviews and audits to ensure that there is conformity between the actual state of a product and the details of its status recorded in the configuration management records.

Close liaison is needed between configuration management and change control. Once a product has been approved, that version of the product never changes. If a change is required, a copy of the product is created with a new version number to incorporate the change. This new version should be linked to documentation about the change which caused the need for the new version.

Quality

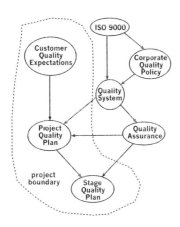

The PRINCE 2 quality path draws together a statement of the customer's quality expectations, the requirements of ISO 9000 and the quality management systems of the customer and supplier to form the Project and Stage Quality Plans. These define quality responsibilities as well as what standards are to be met, plus the methods and techniques to be used. The focus is on project and stage quality planning to ensure that the project delivers to an acceptable level of quality, and plans:

- how each product is to be tested
- when each product is to be tested
- by whom each product is to be tested.

The quality review technique is offered as a procedure to check the quality of any project document. The procedure is linked to Stage Plans and the assurance responsibilities.

A Quality Log provides an audit trail of all the quality work done in a project and encompasses the quality checks done on work contributed by third parties.

Risk

Risk Analysis   **Risk Management**

The management of risk is one of the most important
parts of the Project Manager's and Project Board's jobs.
The Project Manager is responsible for ensuring that
risks are identified, recorded and regularly reviewed.

The Project Board has three responsibilities:

• notifying the Project Manager of the project's exposure
  to any external risks, such as competition or changes in
  company policy
• making decisions on the Project Manager's
  recommended reactions to risks
• striking a balance between level of risk and the cost of
  countermeasures.

In PRINCE 2 risks are controlled by a procedure
summarised in the figure above.

Risk analysis covers:

- risk identification, which determines the potential risks which could be faced by the project
- risk estimation, which determines how important each risk is, based on an assessment of its likelihood and consequences to the project and the business
- risk evaluation, which decides whether the level of a risk is acceptable or not and, if not, what actions can be taken to make it more acceptable.

Risk management consists of four activities:

- planning the countermeasures
- resourcing these countermeasures
- monitoring work on the countermeasures and any changes to the risk
- controlling by taking actions to ensure that the countermeasures are successful.

The management of risk needs to be conducted continuously throughout the project as information becomes available and as circumstances change. In PRINCE 2 risks are formally assessed at Project Initiation, the end of each stage and as part of any exception situation. Risk assessment is also part of the impact analysis of all major change requests.

First published 1997
Fourth impression 1999

ISBN 0 11 330853 1

For further information regarding this and other CCTA
products please contact:
CCTA Library
Rosebery Court
St Andrews Business Park
Norwich NR7 0HS
Telephone: 01603 704930

Printed in the United Kingdom for The Stationery Office
J87460 C60 8/99